First Edition publishe[...]

Copyright © Vicky W[...]

All rights reserved. No [...]
reproduced, distributed [...] in any form or
by any means, including photocopying, recording, or
other electronic or mechanical methods, without the prior
written permission of the publisher, except in the case of
brief quotations embodied in critical reviews and certain
other noncommercial uses permitted by copyright law.
For permission requests, write to the publisher via email,
addressed "Attention: Permissions Coordinator," at the
address below.

Email. vickywoodings@hotmail.com

Illustration and design by Mark Jackson.

Printed in the United Kingdom.

ISBN 978-1-5272-9675-6

To my darling daughter,

I always have been and always will be so proud of you throughout this fight.

Lots of love today, everyday and forever.

Mum x

Annie lived in a lovely
house by the sea,
with her mum, her dad
and her dog Bobby.

She went to a school up
the hill, from 9 until 3,
and she worked very hard,
and was very happy.

She liked travel and art
and was always so kind.
A lovelier girl you'd be
hard pushed to find.

One day, unexpectedly, there was a knock at the door.

Ed appeared asking to come in and sit on the floor.

"I am far too busy with my friends today!"

said the girl and closed the door in *Ed's* way.

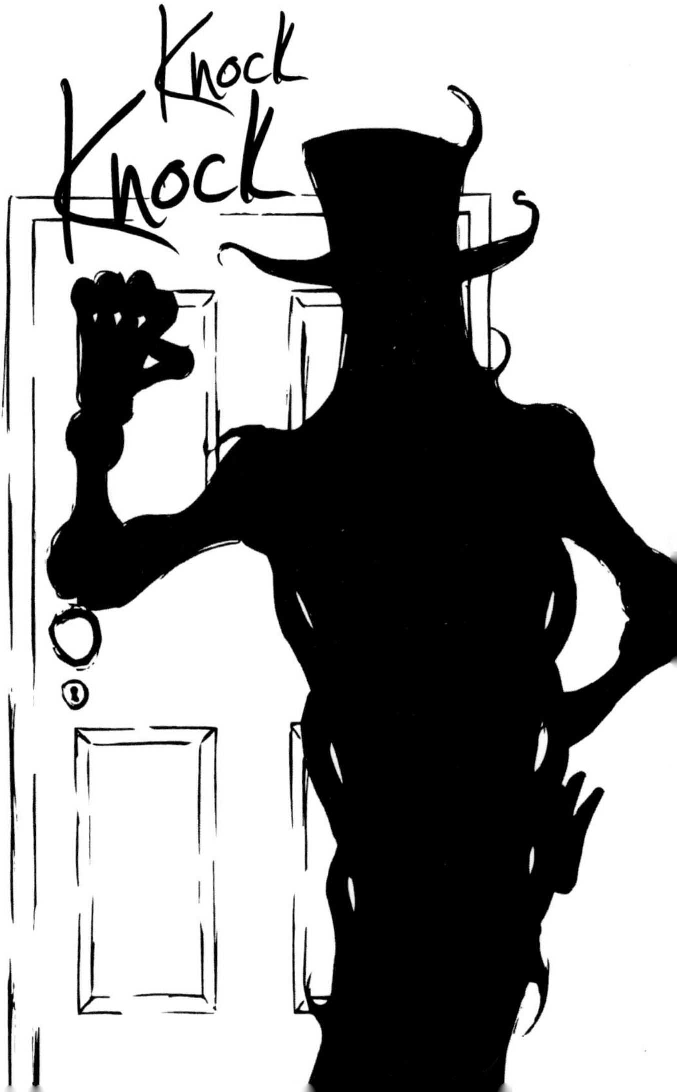
Knock
Knock

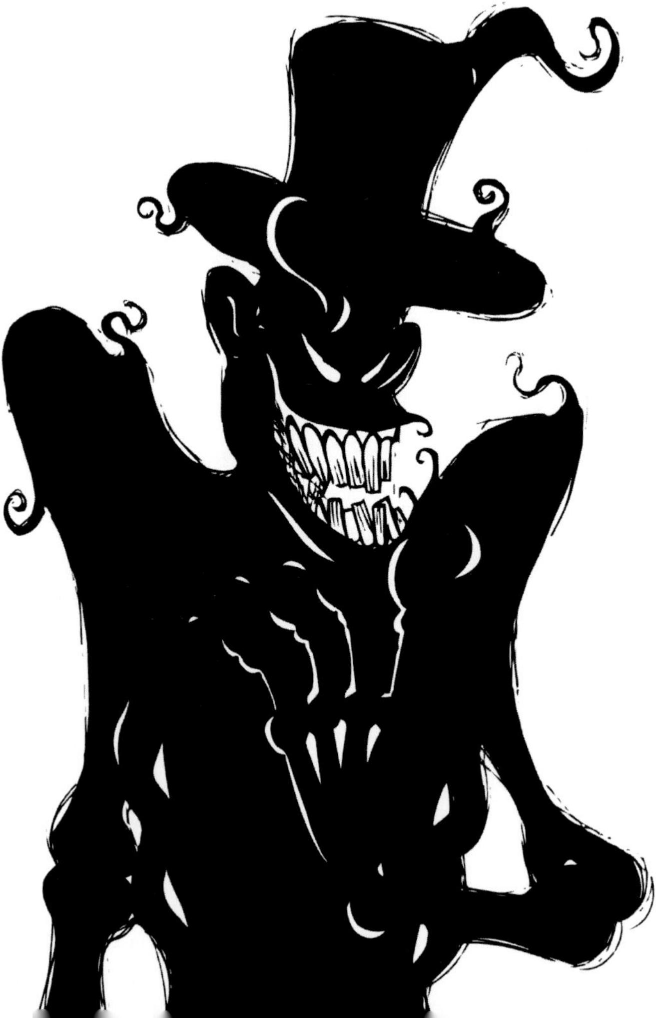

He knocked at the door
again and again.

I will stay as long
as you want me to.

But Annie said,
"No, I don't want you!"

A week later, the unwelcome visitor returned and banged on the door.

"I'm out with my family, go away!"
but *Ed* was determined,
he would knock even more.

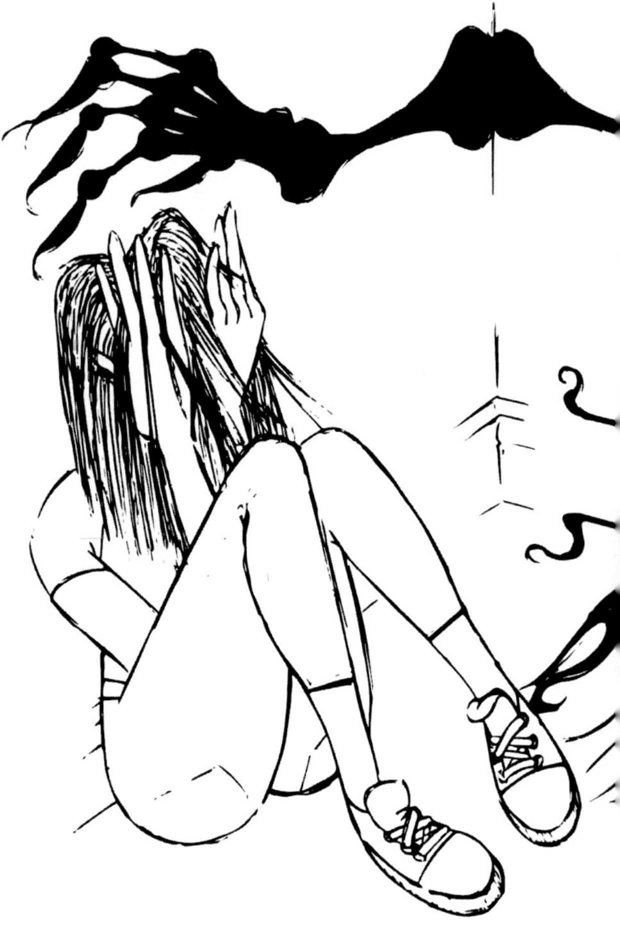

One day *he* knocked so hard
and she opened the door.

Her best friend had been mean
and he sat with her on the floor.

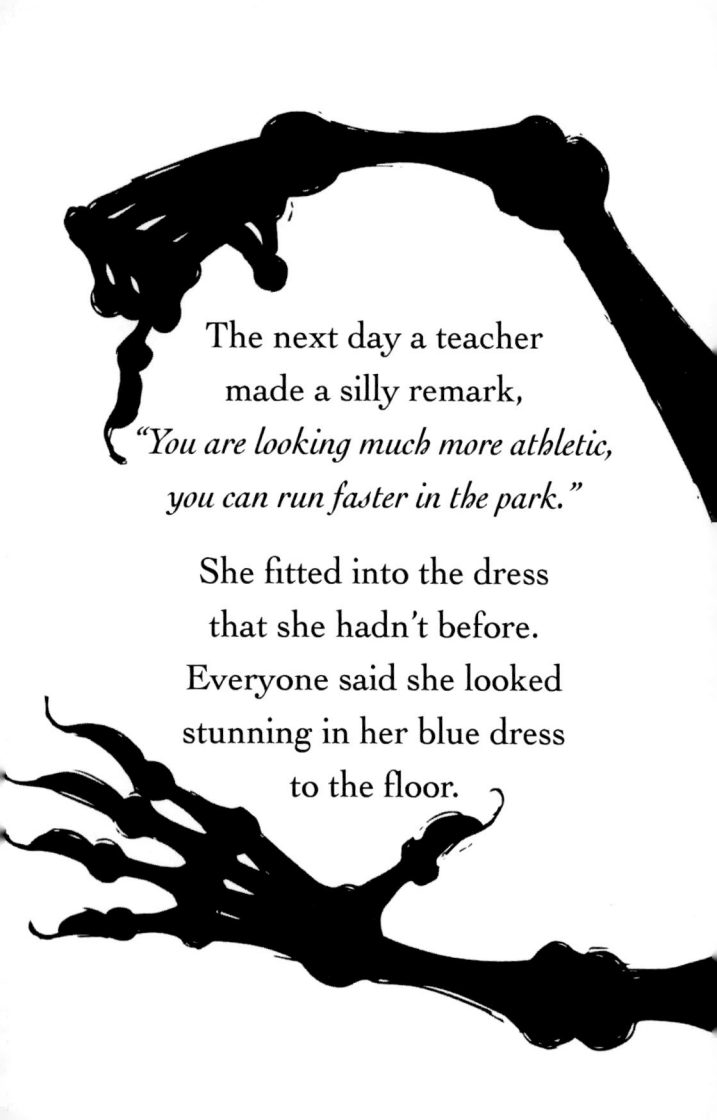

The next day a teacher
made a silly remark,
*"You are looking much more athletic,
you can run faster in the park."*

She fitted into the dress
that she hadn't before.
Everyone said she looked
stunning in her blue dress
to the floor.

A week later, the dentist said, "cut out all sugar!"

Ed's space at the table grew bigger and bigger.

Now *Ed* shared her seat
at the kitchen table,
as *Annie* tried hard to
eat whenever she was able.

He kept coming and coming and *he* made *Annie* sad.

She was scared now and feeling so very bad.

Ed made so many rules and demands that *Annie* couldn't keep up.

She no longer felt safe drinking water from a cup.

The friends that she had were no longer there.

She was just so confused,
and she no longer cared.

The things that she enjoyed
she could no longer remember.

Ed's place at the table was so
big and she was so *slender.*

She could no longer walk
Bobby and watch him play.

She had to rest and tried
to stay out of his way.

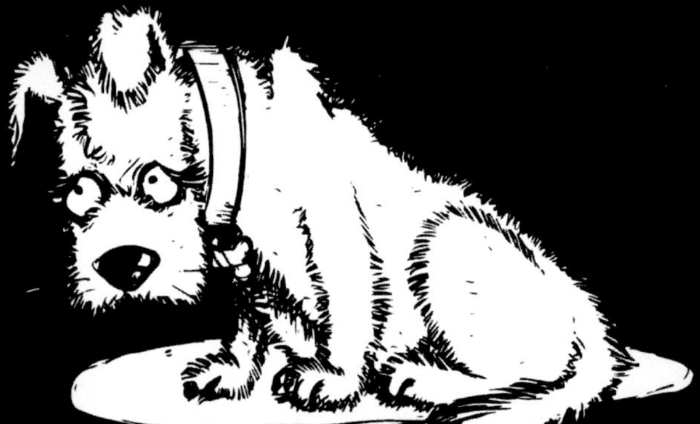

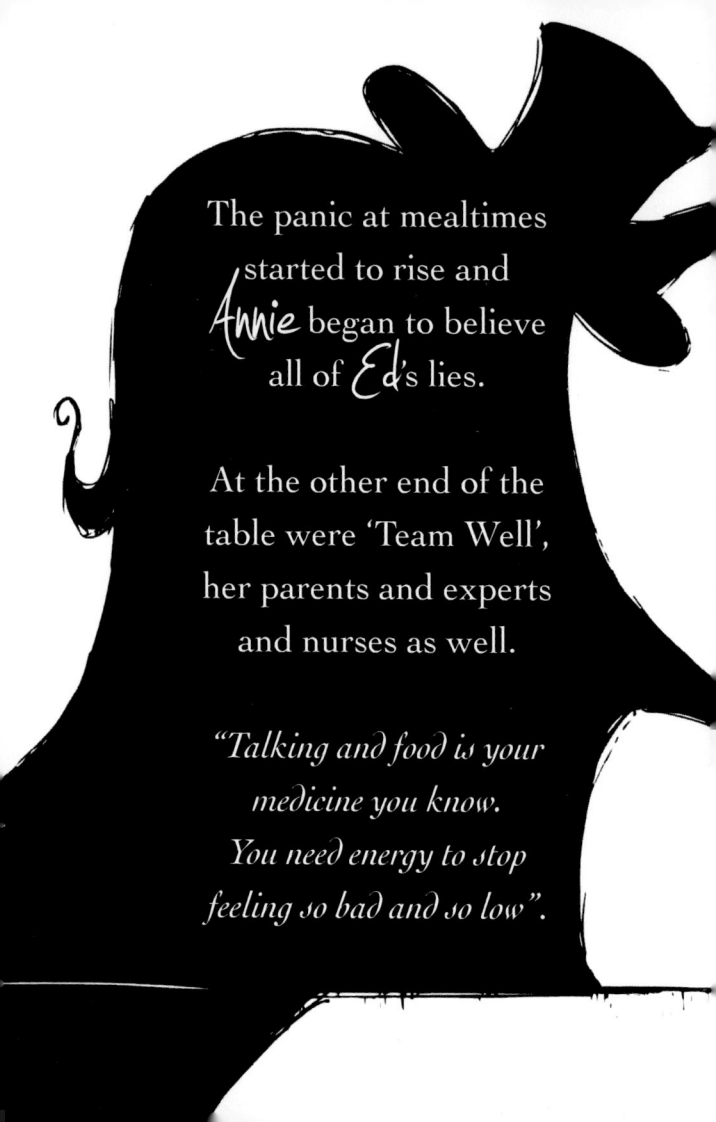

The panic at mealtimes started to rise and *Annie* began to believe all of *Ed*'s lies.

At the other end of the table were 'Team Well', her parents and experts and nurses as well.

"Talking and food is your medicine you know.
You need energy to stop feeling so bad and so low".

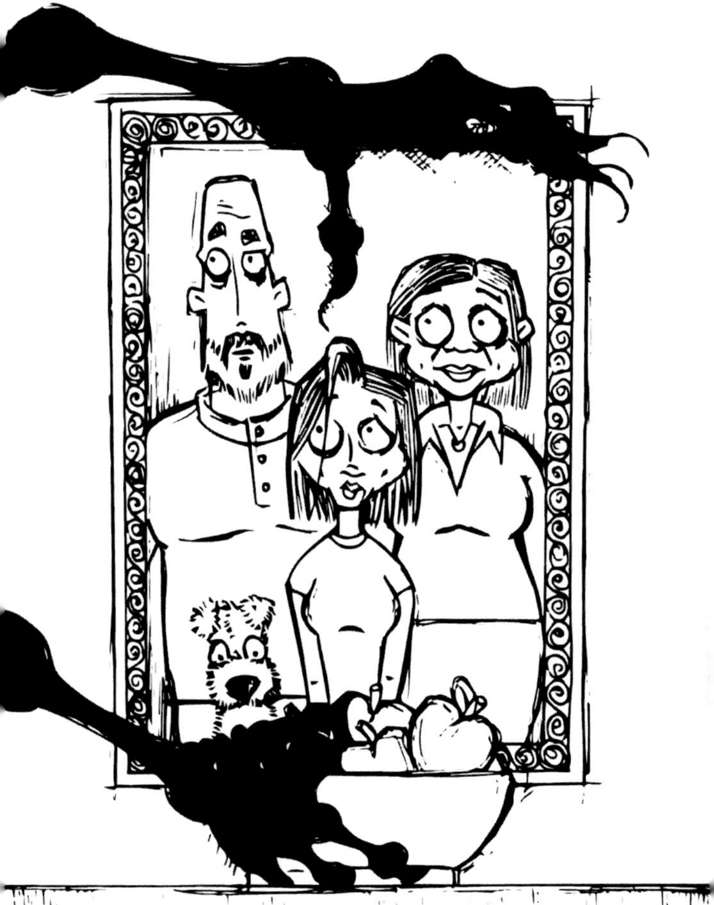

They calmly encouraged
her to take back control
and to see *Ed* as a
monster - an evil troll.

Annie held onto *Ed* as she
thought *he* was her *friend*.
She struggled to see a happier end.

At first there were
only slivers of light
to follow and encourage
her bite after bite.

One day when Annie
awoke *Ed* wasn't as loud.

*"I'm not going to let you
win - you're a bully.
You're unkind and mean -
and I want you gone fully."*

She had good days and bad
days, and it took time to heal.
It was hard to gain strength
and to learn how to feel.

Ed continued to rage and
fought with all his might.
He didn't like Annie
following the light.

Give him an inch and
he would take a mile,
stealing her joy and
taking her smile.

Annie had 'Team Well'
fighting her corner,
holding her hope every
time that she faltered.

On the darkest days
they held her hope high,
encouraging her
to continue to try.

Eventually, one day she
felt like the Annie of old.
She was **healthy** and **strong.**
She was **brave.** She was **bold.**

She didn't need *Ed*
to help her cope,
she clung to her dreams
and her own newfound hope.

Annie thanked all the team
that had played their part,
in recovering her strength
right from the start.

The battle was hard,
and the battle was long,
but Annie was proud
to be healthy and strong.

Ed lurked in the shadows
and waited to knock,

...now there was a healthy bright
key fitted tight in the lock.

Bible
God Make

Sophie Piper ✷ Estelle Corke

LION
CHILDREN'S

Imagine a dark and stormy night.

Imagine a dark and stormy sea.

Before the world began, there was only darkness and storm.

Then God spoke: "Let there be light."

The light shone. God had made the very first day.

On the second day, God spoke again: "Let there be sky above and sea below." And there was.

"Next," said God, "I want land as well as sea."

At once the land appeared. Plants began to grow: some were tiny; some were tall.

"I have worked for three days, and everything is very good," said God.

On day four, God made the sun.
"You must shine through the day,"
said God.

"Moon and the stars: I want you to shine at night."
The whole universe did what God commanded.

Early on the fifth morning, God made all kinds of sea creatures: they came darting and diving through the waves.

Then God made the birds. They flapped and flew in the clear air.

On the sixth day, God made the animals – all kinds of amazing animals.

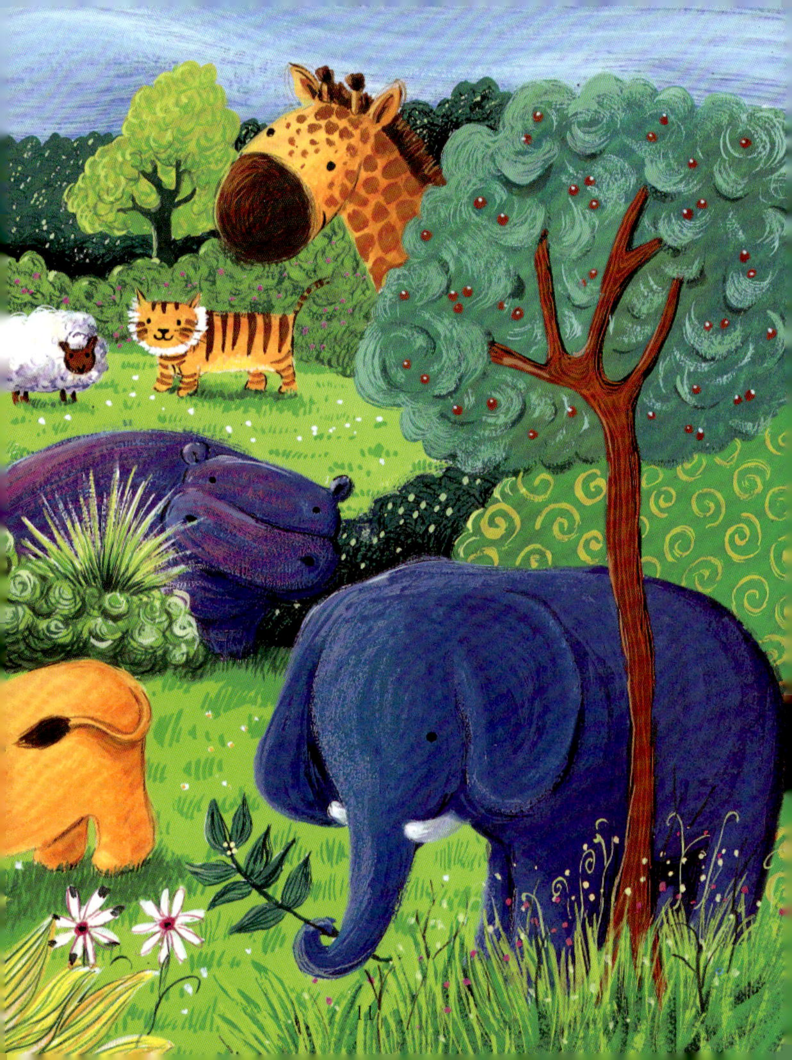

"And last," said God, "I shall make human beings. They will take care of my world."

The six days of making were over.
It was time for a day of rest.

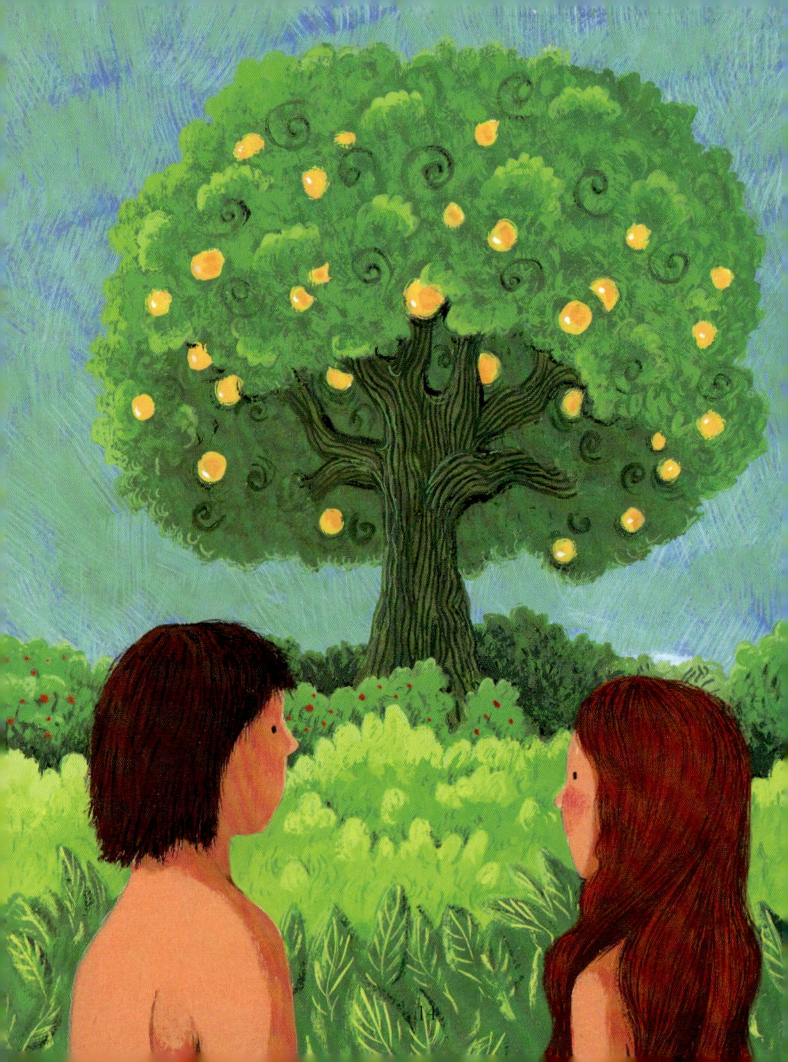

The first man was named Adam.
The first woman was named Eve.
God gave them a garden home.

"Everything is for you," said God. "There is just one tree you must not touch. If you eat its fruit, everything will go wrong."

Adam and Eve were happy in their paradise home.

One day, a snake came and spoke to Eve. "Did God say you mustn't eat the fruit here?" it asked.

"Only the fruit from one tree," replied Eve. "If we eat that, everything will go wrong."

The snake twisted and wriggled. "Not true!" it said. "The fruit will make you as wise as God. Go on. Try it!"

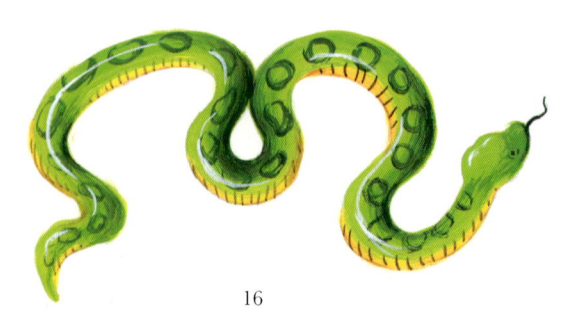

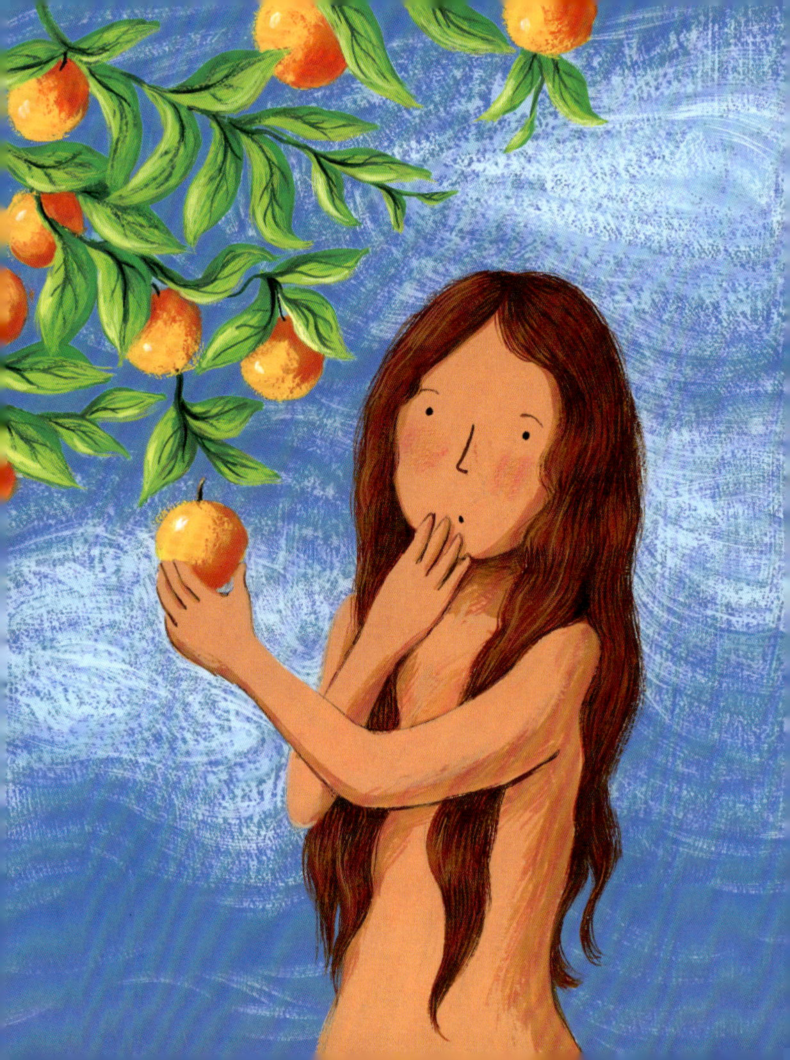

Eve reached up. She picked the forbidden fruit. She ate some.

"It's good," she said. "I shall give some to Adam."

Adam took a bite. Then he and Eve looked at each other.

"Oh dear," they cried.

"We're both naked," said Eve.

"And now, for the first time, that doesn't seem right," said Adam.

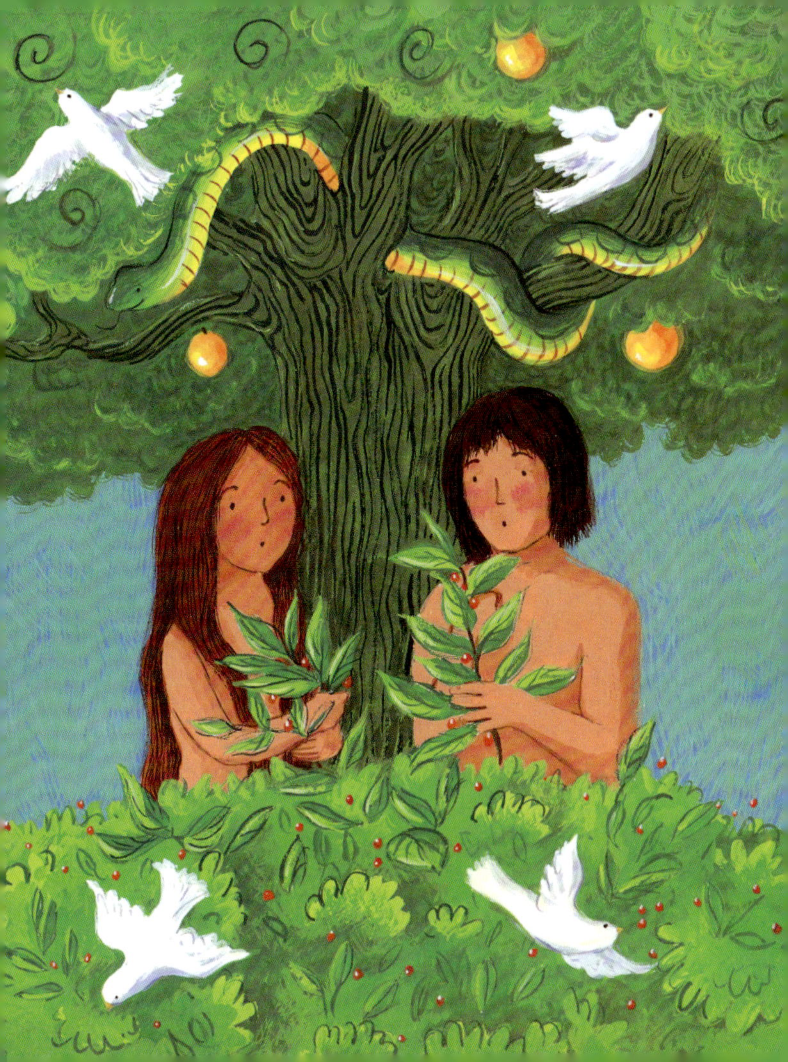

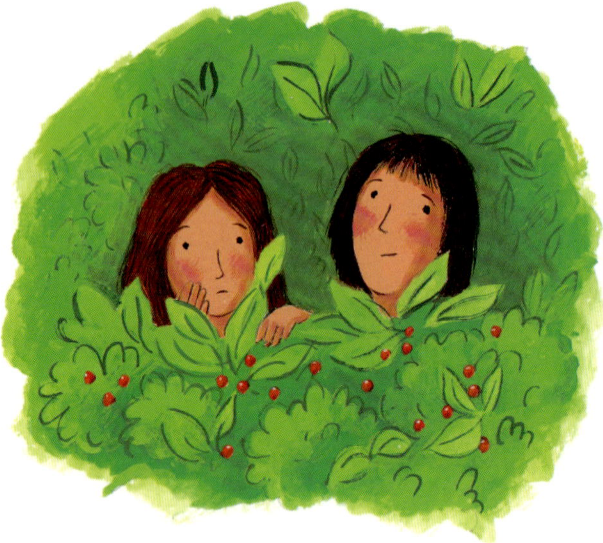

They spent the day making clothes from leaves. Then they heard God coming. They hid among the trees.

God called them.

God found them.

God saw what had happened, and God was sad.

22

"Now everything must change," said God. "You must say goodbye to paradise. You must go out into the wide world. There you will work for all the things you need."

God made Adam and Eve clothes to wear.

Sadly they walked out of the garden.

As they looked back, they saw an angel with a sword. The blade flashed this way and that. They could not go to the garden ever again.

They looked ahead. "There are lots of weeds here," said Adam. "But if we work hard, we can plant crops. We'll manage."

Eve wiped away a tear. "It's sad not being friends with God," she said. "I hope this mistake is put right one day."